The Dweller On The Threshold:

Earthbound Spirits

Max Heindel

PART III.

"The Dweller on the Threshold"

Earth-bound Spirits

WHILE we are studying "The Web of Destiny, How Made and Unmade," it is expedient that we devote some time to the mysterious "Dweller on the Threshold," a subject that is quite misunderstood. Our investigations of the previous lives of a number of people who have applied to the Fellowship headquarters for relief from so-called obsession, have proved that their trouble is due to one phase of what has been mistakenly called by previous investigators, "The Dweller on the Threshold." When cases are examined merely by the use of spiritual sight or by reading in the etheric record, such a mistake may very easily be made as to confuse that apparition with the true Dweller on the Threshold. But as soon as we look the cases up in the imperishable records contained in the Region of Archetypal Forces, the matter is at once cleared up and the facts developed in these investigations may be summed up as follows:

At the moment of death when the seed atom in the heart is ruptured which contains all the experience of the past life in a panoramic picture, the spirit leaves its physical body taking with it the finer bodies. It then hovers over the dense body which is now dead, as we call it, for a time varying from a number of hours to three and one half days. The determining factor as to the time is the strength of the vital body, the vehicle which constitutes the soul body spoken of in the Bible. There is then a pictorial reproduction of the life, a panorama in reverse order from death to birth, and the pictures are etched upon the desire body through the medium of the reflecting ether in this vital body. During this time the consciousness of the Spirit is concentrated in the vital body, or at least it should be, and it has therefore no feeling about this matter. The picture that is impressed upon the vehicle of feeling and emotion, the desire body, is the basis of subsequent suffering in the life in Purgatory for evil deeds, and of enjoyment in the first Heaven on account of the good done in the past life.

These were the main facts which the writer was able to personally observe about death at the time when the teachings were first given to him and when he was introduced by the help of the Teacher to the panoramic reproductions of life when persons were going through the gate of death, but the investigations of later years have revealed the additional fact that there is another process going on during these important days following death. A cleavage takes place in the vital body similar to that made by the process of initiation. So much of this vehicle as can be termed "soul," coalesces with the higher vehicles and is the basis of consciousness in the invisible worlds after death. The lower part, which is discarded, returns to the physical body and hovers over the grave in the great majority of cases, as stated in the Cosmo. This cleavage of the vital body is not the same in all persons but depends upon the nature of the life lived and the character of the person that is passing out. In extreme cases this division varies very much from normal. This important point was brought out in many cases of supposed spirit obsession which have been investigated from headquarters; in fact it was these cases which developed the far-reaching and astounding discoveries brought out by our most recent researches into the nature of the obsession from which the people who appealed to us were suffering. As might be expected, of course, the division in these cases showed a preponderance of evil, and efforts were then made to find out if there were not also another class of people where a different division with a preponderance of good takes place. It is a pleasure to record that this was found to be the case, and after weighing the facts discovered, balancing one with another, the following seems to be a correct description of the conditions and their reason:

The vital body aims to build the physical, whereas our desires and emotions tear down. It is the struggle between the vital body and the desire body which produces consciousness in the physical world, and which hardens the tissues so that the soft body of the child gradually becomes tough and shrunken in old age, followed by death. The morality or immorality of our desires and emotions acts in a similar manner on the vital body. Where devotion to high ideals is the mainspring of action, where the devotional nature has been allowed for years to express itself freely and frequently, and particularly where this has been accompanied by the scientific exercises given probationers in the Rosicrucian Fellowship, the quantity of the chemical and life ethers gradually diminishes as the animal appetites vanish, and an increased amount of the light and reflecting ether takes their place. As a consequence, physical health is not as robust among people who follow the higher path as among people whose indulgence of the lower nature attracts the chemical and life ethers, in proportion to the extent and nature of their vice, to the partial or total exclusion of the two higher ethers.

Several very important consequences connected with death follow this fact. As it is the chemical ether which cements the molecules of the body in their places and keeps them there during life, when only a minimum of this material is present, disintegration of the physical vehicle after death must be very rapid. This the writer has not been able to verify because it is difficult to find men of high spiritual proclivities who have passed out recently, but it would seem that this is so from the fact recorded in the Bible that the body of Christ was not found in the tomb when the people came to look for it. As we have said before in relation to this matter, the Christ spiritualized the body of Jesus so highly, made it so vibrant, that it was almost impossible to keep the particles in place during his ministry. This was a fact known to the writer by the teachings of the Elder Brothers and by what investigation he has made of the subject in the Memory of Nature, but the bearing of this fact upon the general subject of death and the after-existence was not known until lately.

The real "Dweller on the Threshold" is the composite elemental entity created on the invisible planes by all our untransmuted evil thoughts and acts during all the past period of our evolution. This "dweller" stands guard at the entrance to the invisible worlds and challenges our right to enter therein. This entity must be redeemed or transmuted eventually. We must generate poise and will power sufficient to face and command it before we can consciously enter the super-physical worlds.

As before stated, a worldly life increases the proportion of the lower ethers in the vital body to that of the higher. Where, in addition, a so-called "clean life" is lived and excesses avoided, the health during life is more robust than that of the aspirant to the higher life, because the latter's attitude to life builds a vital body composed principally of the higher ethers. He loves "the bread of life" more than physical sustenance, and therefore his instrument becomes increasingly high-strung, nervous, and delicate, a sensitive condition which greatly furthers the objects of the spirit, but which is a hardship from the physical viewpoint.

In the great majority of mankind there is such a preponderance of selfishness and a desire to get the most out of life as they view that matter, that either they are busy keeping the wolf from the door or accumulating possessions and taking care of them, and hence they have very little time or inclination to undertake the soul culture so necessary to true success in life. The writer has often heard them contend that if they pay the minister to study the Bible during the six days and give them on the seventh an epitome of what he has found, that should be all that is required to get a ticket to heaven. They subscribe to the church and do the things ordinarily called for in life as honorable and upright; for the rest, they have "a good time." Therefore there is so little that persists in each life of the majority and evolution is so frightfully slow that until one is able to view the act of death from the higher regions of the World of Concrete Thought and, so to say, look downwards, it does not appear that anything is saved of the vital body. This body seems to return complete to the physical body and to hover over the grave, there to disintegrate simultaneously with the latter. As a matter of fact, an increasing part cleaves to the higher vehicles and goes with them into the desire world, there to be a basis of consciousness in, and to live through, the purgatorial and heaven lives, generally persisting until man enters the second heaven and unites with the nature forces there in his efforts to create for himself a new environment. By that time, it has been absorbed by the spirit or almost so, and whatever may remain of a material nature will quickly fade away. Thus the personality of the past life has vanished and the spirit will not meet with it in the future lives upon this earth.

But there are some people who are of such an evil nature that they *enjoy* a life spent in vice and degenerate practices, a brutal life, and who delight in giving pain. Sometimes they even cultivate the occult arts for evil purposes so that they may have a greater power over their victims. Then their fiendish, immoral practices result in hardening their vital body.

In such extreme cases where the animal nature has been paramount, where there has been no soul expression in the preceding earth life, the division in the vital body spoken of before cannot take place at death, for there is no dividing line. In such a case, if the vital body should gravitate back to the dense body and there gradually disintegrate, the effect of a very evil life would not be so far-reaching, but unfortunately there is in such cases an interlocking grip of the vital and desire bodies which prevents separation. We have seen that where a man lives mostly in the higher nature, his spiritual vehicles are nourished to the detriment of the lower. Conversely, where his consciousness is centered in the lower vehicles, he strengthens them immeasurably. It should be understood that the life of the desire body is not terminated by the departure of the spirit; it has a residual life and consciousness. The vital body is also able to sense things in a slight measure for a few days after death in ordinary cases (hence the suffering caused by embalming, postmortem examinations, etc., immediately after death), but where a low life has hardened and endued it with great strength, it has a tenacious hold on life and an ability to feed on odors of foods and liquors. Sometimes, as a parasite, it even vampirizes people with whom it comes in contact.

Thus an evil man may live for many, many years unseen in our very midst, yet so close that he is nearer than hands and feet. He is far more dangerous than the physical criminal for he is able to prompt others of a similar bent to criminal or degenerate practices without fear of detection or punishment by law.

Such beings are therefore one of the greatest menaces to society imaginable. They have sent countless victims to prison, broken up homes and caused an unbelievable amount of unhappiness. They always leave their victims when the latter have come into the clutches of the law. They gloat over their victims' sorrow and distress, this being a part of their fiendish scheme. There are other classes which delight in posing as "angels" in spiritualistic seances. They also find victims there and teach them immoral practices. The so-called "Poltergeist" which enjoys breaking dishes, upsetting tables, knocking hats over the heads of the delighted audience, and similar horseplay, is also in this class. The strength and density of the vital body of such beings makes it easier for them to give physical manifestations than for those who have passed beyond into the desire world; in fact, the vital bodies of this class of spirits are so dense that they are nearly physical, and it has been a mystery to the writer that some of the people who are taken in by such entities cannot see them. Were they once discovered, one look at their evil sneering faces would very soon dispel the delusion that they are angels.

There is another class of spirits belonging to this same category who appeal to persons seeking spiritual development outside the spiritualistic line, by posing to them as *individual teachers* and giving them a lot of goody-goody nonsense. They also play upon the credulity of their victims in an almost unbelievable manner, and even though for years they may keep their intentions secret, sometime or other they will show themselves in their true colors. Therefore it cannot be reiterated too often that no one should accept from any one else, either visible or invisible, teachings in the slightest degree contrary to his own highest conception of ethics. It is dangerous to trust absolutely to people in this world and admit them to our full confidence; we know this by experience and act accordingly. We ought, naturally, to be much more careful when the question comes to matters of the soul, and not trust that most important of all matters, our spiritual welfare, in the hands of some one we cannot at least see and judge accordingly. There are many spirits, of course, who have not the wits to do anything very evil with their victims, and who just lead them around by the nose for years and years without any particularly harmful results. But *self reliance* is the most essential virtue to be cultivated by us at this stage of our evolution; the mystic maxim, "If thou art Christ, help thyself," is always sounded in the ears of those who endeavor to tread the true path. Hence we ought to guide ourselves without fear or favor from any spirit.

It is amazing when one searches the Memory of Nature of the past to find how prevalent this interlocking condition of the desire and vital bodies was in former centuries and millenniums. We realize, of course, in a sort of an abstract way, that the further we go back into the history of men the more savage we find them, but that in our own historical times this savagery should have been so common and so brutal and that might was the measure of right absolutely and beyond dispute, was, to say the least, quite a shock to the writer. It has been taught that selfishness and desire were purposely fostered under the regime of Jehovah to give incentive to action. This in the course of time had so hardened the desire body that when the advent of Christ took place, there was almost no heaven life among the people then living; but the writer, personally, never realized what this fact implied until the recent investigations of "The Web of Destiny" were commenced.

Nor were these ancient people content to do all the evil they could in life and then get away, but they must even have their war horses killed, their weapons laid down in their coffins, and everything else possible done to keep them here, for the ether in those things which had belonged to them during life had an attraction for them, and was a means to further keeping them within the earth's sphere. It enabled them to haunt, for they actually did haunt, their castles for years and years, and of course it was not only the rich or the warrior classes but also others. In cases of blood feuds where people were slain, the ghosts incited their relatives to avenge them by remaining about and helping them to carry out the bloody deeds. Thus they perpetuated evil and kept the world in a turmoil of blood and strife; nor is this condition entirely broken in what we call modern days. Wherever a person dies who has fostered malice and hatred in his heart, these interlock the desire and vital bodies and make him a more serious menace to the community than anyone can imagine who has not investigated this subject. Therefore, if for no other reason, capital punishment should be abolished so that we may not let loose upon the community such dangerous characters to incite the morally weak to follow in their footsteps.

CPSIA information can be obtained
at www.ICGtesting.com
Printed in the USA
LVHW101125100220
646337LV00026BA/145